ZIMBABWE

...in Pictures

Visual Geography Series®

ZIMBABWE

...in Pictures

Prepared by
Thomas O'Toole

Lerner Publications Company
Minneapolis

Independent Picture Service

**Prehistoric inhabitants of Zimbabwe drew these images
of giraffes – animals that still roam the country.**

This is an all-new edition of the Visual Geography
Series. Previous editions have been published by
Sterling Publishing Company, New York City. The
text, set in 10/12 Century Textbook, is fully revised
and updated, and new photographs, maps, charts, and
captions have been added.

LIBRARY OF CONGRESS CATALOGING-IN-PUBLICATION DATA

O'Toole, Thomas, 1941–
   Zimbabwe in pictures.

   (Visual geography series)
   Previous ed. published as: Rhodesia in pictures.
   Includes index.
   Summary: Introduces the land, history, government,
people, and economy of one of Africa's most controver-
sial countries.
   1. Zimbabwe. [1. Zimbabwe] I. Title. II. Series:
Visual geography series (Minneapolis, Minn.)
DT962.086   1987   968.91   87-21348
ISBN 0-8225-1825-2 (lib. bdg.)

International Standard Book Number: 0-8225-1825-2
Library of Congress Catalog Card Number: 87-21348

VISUAL GEOGRAPHY SERIES®

Publisher
Harry Jonas Lerner
Associate Publisher
Nancy M. Campbell
Senior Editor
Mary M. Rodgers
Editor
Gretchen Bratvold
Editorial Assistant
Nora W. Kniskern
Illustrations Editor
Karen A. Sirvaitis
Consultants/Contributors
Thomas O'Toole
John H. Peck
Sandra K. Davis
Designer
Jim Simondet
Cartographer
Carol F. Barrett
Indexer
Kristine I. Spangard
Production Manager
Gary J. Hansen

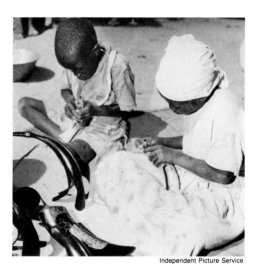
Independent Picture Service

**These children supplement their family's income by
making handicrafts.**

Acknowledgments

Title page photo by Amandus Schneider.

Elevation contours adapted from *The Times Atlas of
the World*, seventh comprehensive edition (New York:
Times Books, 1985).

4 5 6 7 8 9 10 – JR – 03 02 01 00 99 98 97

Independent Picture Service

Accompanied by their children, rural Zimbabwean women collect water and wash clothes in local streams.

Contents

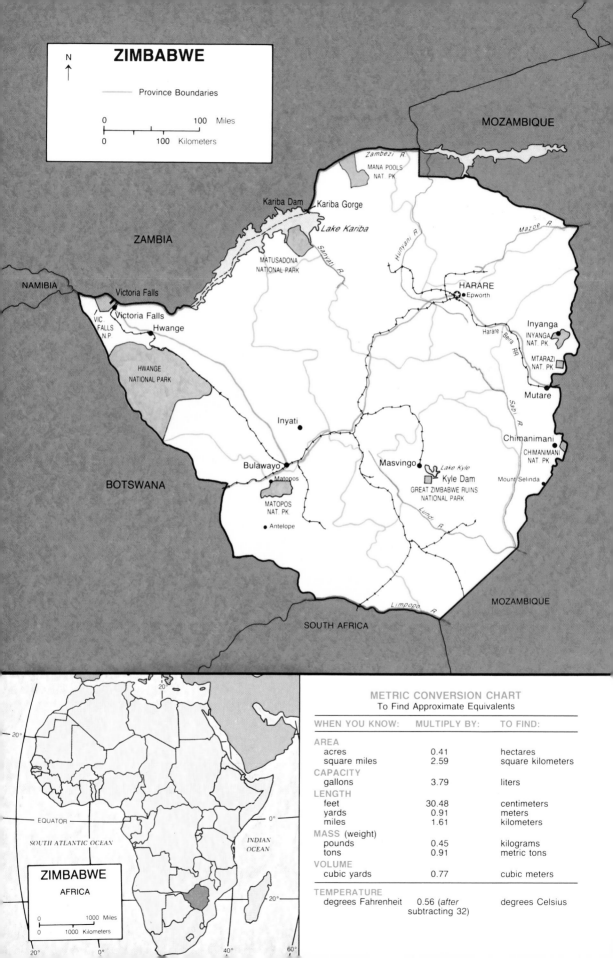

ZIMBABWE

Province Boundaries

0   100   Miles

0   100   Kilometers

N

MOZAMBIQUE

ZAMBIA

Zambezi R.

MANA POOLS
NAT. PK.

Kariba Dam   Kariba Gorge

Lake Kariba

Mazoe R.

MATUSADONA
NATIONAL PARK

Sanyati R.

Hunyani R.

HARARE
● Epworth

NAMIBIA

Victoria Falls

Victoria Falls

VIC.
FALLS
N.P.

Hwange

Inyanga

INYANGA
NAT. PK.

Harare Bera RR

MTARAZI
NAT. PK.

HWANGE
NATIONAL PARK

Sabi R.

Mutare

Inyati

Chimanimani

CHIMANIMANI
NAT. PK.

Bulawayo

Matopos

Masvingo

Lake Kyle

Kyle Dam

Mount Selinda

BOTSWANA

MATOPOS
NAT. PK.

GREAT ZIMBABWE RUINS
NATIONAL PARK

● Antelope

Lundi R.

MOZAMBIQUE

Limpopo R.

SOUTH AFRICA

EQUATOR

SOUTH ATLANTIC OCEAN

INDIAN
OCEAN

ZIMBABWE

AFRICA

0   1000 Miles

0   1000 Kilometers

METRIC CONVERSION CHART
To Find Approximate Equivalents

WHEN YOU KNOW:	MULTIPLY BY:	TO FIND:
AREA		
acres	0.41	hectares
square miles	2.59	square kilometers
CAPACITY		
gallons	3.79	liters
LENGTH		
feet	30.48	centimeters
yards	0.91	meters
miles	1.61	kilometers
MASS (weight)		
pounds	0.45	kilograms
tons	0.91	metric tons
VOLUME		
cubic yards	0.77	cubic meters
TEMPERATURE		
degrees Fahrenheit	0.56 (*after* subtracting 32)	degrees Celsius

In limestone caves near Harare, trapped water creates vivid, blue pools.

Introduction

Zimbabwe took its name from the ruins of Great Zimbabwe (meaning venerated house), which lie near Masvingo. In choosing a name from the Shona language—one of Zimbabwe's main tongues—Zimbabwe proudly proclaimed its ties to an age-old history of achievement and settlement of black peoples in southern Africa. Prior to its official emergence in 1980 as an independent republic, the territory was dubbed Rhodesia—after the ambitious British financier, Cecil Rhodes—by its white, colonial population.

Not everyone is happy with the awakening of black African pride that is evident throughout Zimbabwe. Some white Zimbabweans—particularly those who are of the last colonial-era generation—continue to have negative views about the way the black majority runs the country. At the same time, some black Zimbabweans resent the way the white minority continues to dominate the economy. Both black and white nationalists are quick to blame government shortcomings on colonial policies, which controlled development of the area for nearly a century.

Despite Zimbabwe's internal problems and racial tensions, the country is blessed with promising natural riches. On a purely material level, fertile land, abundant mineral wealth, huge potential energy resources, and budding industries encourage economic optimism. The beauty of the Zimbabwean countryside and the heritage of the nation's many peoples—from all ethnic groups—form a strong cultural fabric. Zimbabwe stands out as an African nation where people of all colors, cultures, and creeds have their own importance, and where the future promises great accomplishments.

A bridge spans this narrow section of the Zambezi River, which separates Zimbabwe from neighboring Zambia.

1) The Land

The landlocked Republic of Zimbabwe lies in south central Africa. The country may seem comparatively small, but its area of 150,820 square miles makes it nearly as large as California. The boundaries of Zimbabwe generally lie where natural barriers exist. To the north, for example, the Zambezi River separates Zimbabwe from Zambia. The Limpopo River forms Zimbabwe's southern boundary, which separates the nation from neighboring Botswana and South Africa. Mozambique's border lies to the east and north of Zimbabwe, along the path of the Eastern Highlands.

The Plains

Zimbabwe is part of a great plateau that dominates southern Africa. The central part of Zimbabwe's section of this plateau—called the High Veld (*veld* is the Afrikaans word for plain)—is a giant hump that stretches 400 miles north and south and 50 miles west and east. On either side of this hump extends the Middle Veld, or grassland, at an elevation of 2,000 to 4,000 feet above sea level. Deep river valleys split this area into great expanses of flat countryside. The Low Veld, which is less than 2,000 feet above sea level, consists of a narrow strip in the Zambezi Valley and a broader tract between the Limpopo and Sabi rivers. The lowest point in the country, only 660 feet above sea level, is in the extreme south, where the Limpopo continues into South Africa.

The Eastern Highlands

Along Zimbabwe's eastern border with Mozambique lies a belt of mountain ranges collectively called the Eastern Highlands. The highlands not only form a natural boundary but are also a major watershed, or drainage area, for the region's rivers and streams.

The peaks of the Vumba Mountains—located in the center of this long highland belt—rise to heights of several thousand feet. To the north of this range are the Inyanga Mountains, where Mount Inyangani—Zimbabwe's highest point—rises to 8,514 feet. In this region archaeologists have found traces of early human communities in the form of stone tools and containers, which were used in hunting and cooking and which reflected their settled lifestyle.

Rivers

Two rivers flow along Zimbabwe's northern and southern borders—the Zambezi and the Limpopo, respectively. The Zambezi, Africa's fourth longest river, flows east through Lake Kariba, which was created by the Kariba Dam. Eventually, the river runs

Courtesy of John H. Peck

The Matopo Hills lie in the High Veld, about 25 miles from the city of Bulawayo.

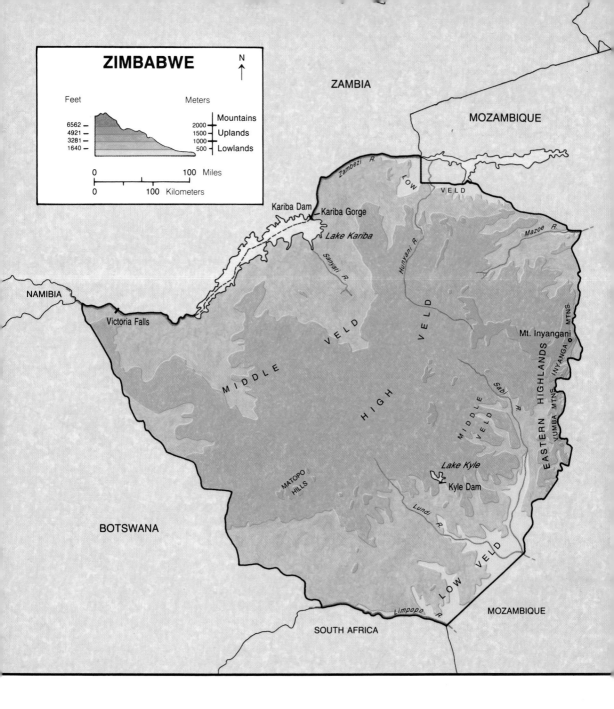

into the Mozambique Channel and empties into the Indian Ocean. Within Zimbabwe, the Sanyati River flows into the Zambezi and drains the interior of the country.

The Limpopo travels east toward Mozambique along Zimbabwe's southern border. The Sabi and Lundi rivers—which water south central regions of Zimbabwe —begin in the High Veld and flow south-eastward through Mozambique to the Indian Ocean.

Great Zimbabwe

The ruins of Great Zimbabwe, one of the most important archaeological sites in southern Africa, are located in south-eastern Zimbabwe near Masvingo (once

Great Zimbabwe was built in stages over several centuries and served as a fortified center of trading and religious activity. Architects designed the walls *(above)* to take advantage of natural barriers, such as large boulders. The outer walls *(lower left)* were curved and decorated at the top with geometric carvings. Inside *(lower right)*, the pathways were narrow between thick walls. No mortar was used to build the enclosure; workers cut and fit the stones tightly together in an intricate pattern.

known as Fort Victoria). This city of religious and royal buildings dates from at least A.D. 1250 and is estimated to have once served a population of more than 10,000 people. Built of stone with no mortar, the walls range in thickness from 3 to 15 feet and in some places are 20 feet high.

The stone structures of Great Zimbabwe were built by Shona-speaking peoples who had established trading contacts with commercial centers on Africa's southeastern coast. Trading locally mined gold and other valuable items, the rulers of Great Zimbabwe imported a wide variety of goods a long time before Portuguese merchants arrived on the coast in the sixteenth century. Pottery, iron tools, gold and copper ornaments, and stone carvings, as well as Persian, Indian, and Chinese ar-

ticles, have been excavated at this and other sites in the country.

Victoria Falls

When the Zambezi River system – swollen with the rains that begin in October – reaches Victoria Falls, the waterway is 1.25 miles wide. Its powerful volume of water hurtles down a 350-foot chasm and sends smokelike spray 1,500 feet into the air. During times of flooding, the local name for the falls—Mosiatunya, meaning "the smoke that thunders"—is especially fitting. These magnificent falls on the northwestern Zimbabwe-Zambia border form one of the most impressive sights in all of Africa. Every April, 75 million gallons of water flow over the falls each minute, creating a thick mist.

Photo by Amandus Schneider

As the rain-swollen Zambezi River crashes into a deep chasm at Victoria Falls, a heavy mist sprays upward creating a smokelike effect.

Photo by Amandus Schneider

Victoria Falls are over a mile wide, but each section *(one is shown above)* demonstrates the immense power of the water volume. At the end of the rift, the Zambezi River travels through a narrow gorge to continue its journey east to Mozambique.

Kariba Dam and Lake Kariba

The name Kariba comes from the Shona word *kariwa,* meaning "a little trap," and refers to the fact that the Zambezi River narrows at the Kariba Gorge. In order to provide hydroelectric power for industry in south central Africa, the Kariba Dam was built in 1959 across the Zambezi River some distance below Victoria Falls. Lake Kariba, which was formed by the dam, became the largest artificial lake in the world at the time, covering 2,050 square miles. (It now takes second place to the reservoir of the Bratsk Dam in Russia.)

When the dam wall was completed and the waters of the Zambezi River began to rise higher and higher, a tremendous effort was made to save the animals that had lived on the land that was being flooded. People from all over the world sent vast sums of money to help in the huge rescue work, which was called "Operation Noah." Smaller animals were caught in nets and transported by boat to dry land. Elephants

Courtesy of Earl Scott

Through the thick mist at Victoria Falls, rainbows frequently appear.

13

Built between 1955 and 1959, the Kariba Dam rises to over 400 feet in height and spans 2,000 feet of the Zambezi River.

Lake Kariba was formed in 1960–1961 when the Kariba Dam became fully operational. About 50,000 people were resettled, and countless animals were evacuated when the waters diverted from the Zambezi River flooded their homes and habitats.

and other kinds of large game were herded into the water and assisted in their long swim ashore.

Many workers from Botswana, Mozambique, and even Italy joined the Zimbabweans in constructing the dam. It was a dangerous undertaking, and about 300 workers lost their lives during the five-year period of its construction.

Lake Kariba—which is 175 miles long and 20 miles across at its widest point— is in the heart of a fertile region. The lake resembles a saltwater sea rather than a freshwater body. Jellyfish, plankton, and shrimp live in it, and gulls and terns fly overhead and dive for small fish. The establishment of a permanent source of water has led to an increase in the animal and bird life on the shores of the lake. Herds of elephants and many species of antelope regularly visit the lake in their migratory searches for food and water.

Wildlife

Large numbers of elephants, lions, leopards, rhinoceroses, hippopotamuses, zebras, giraffes, buffalo, and antelope are still found in Zimbabwe. The nation's wide and colorful array of animals also includes hyenas, cheetahs, and numerous varieties of deer.

Many of the smaller endangered species, such as the aardwolf (related to the hyena) and the pangolin—or scaly anteater—are given special protection. Also found in Zimbabwe are the vervet monkey, the striped polecat, and the clawless otter. Altogether, 168 species of mammals are found in the country.

Zimbabwe also has a spectacular number of birds. For example, there are 8 species of robins, 11 kinds of cuckoos, 13 sorts of swallows, and 17 different eagles. Brightly feathered birds include red-breasted shrikes, green and purple lories, bee-eaters, and waxbills. Songbirds such as buntings, warblers, canaries, and finches enliven the air with their pleasant calls.

Photo by Amandus Schneider

A cluster of sable antelope represents a nearly extinct species that is preserved in Zimbabwe. The animals are distinguished by their large, curved horns and glossy, black coats.

Photo by Amandus Schneider

Semi-aquatic hippos spend much of the daytime immersed in water. As evening approaches, however, they often emerge in search of land plants to supplement their diet, which depends heavily on river vegetation.

Largest of the country's many protected areas, Hwange National Park covers over three million acres in eastern Zimbabwe. Its huge concentrations of animals, including herds of eland – the biggest African antelope – roam freely in search of pasturelands.

Numerous game parks have been established both to help conserve animal life and to provide a means of viewing the creatures in their native habitats. Eleven areas of Zimbabwe, totaling over three million acres, have been declared national parks. The national parks at Victoria Falls, Inyanga, Mtarazi, Chimanimani, and Matopos are famous areas of exceptional scenic beauty. Other regions—such as Matusadona and Hwange—are mainly wildlife areas, where Zimbabwe's wild animals can live and multiply in safety.

Climate

Since Zimbabwe lies just north of the Tropic of Capricorn, it might be thought of as a land of tropical heat. Because of its altitude, however, Zimbabwe has one of the most moderate climates in the world, with no extremes of heat or cold. In addition to its altitude, the country's inland location helps to prevent excessive humidity.

Located in the Southern Hemisphere, Zimbabwe has seasons that are the reverse of those in the United States or Europe. Officially, Zimbabwe has only a rainy and a

Near Bulawayo in southern Zimbabwe lies Matopos National Park, where these cheetahs climb the rock-strewn hillsides to sight fresh game.

dry season, but there are small yet noticeable changes each month. The rains bring a freshened atmosphere and lush vegetation to all areas and altitudes. As the rainless months progress, these effects lessen gradually until the countryside becomes brown and dry. The rains always come again, but if they come too late, drought can cause serious damage to all crops. The economy, which is largely agricultural, can be seriously affected at such times.

Cities

Harare, the capital of Zimbabwe, has many of the features of urban centers in Europe or the United States, including skyscrapers and well-kept parks. Harare is often called "the city of flowering trees" because of its abundance of vibrant blossoms. Purple-hued jacaranda, red royal poinciana, and pink bauhinia trees brighten the city's appearance.

In less than a century, the capital has grown from flat prairie land to a sophisticated city of more than 1.2 million people. On September 12, 1890, the Pioneer Column—as the first white settlers were known—camped on an open plain at the end of their long journey from what was called Bechuanaland (present-day Botswana). A garden surrounded by modern commercial buildings now stands on the spot where the pioneers first raised a simple flagpole. Since those early years, Harare—then called Salisbury—has served as the nation's administrative hub. It also acts as the main distribution point of the area's agricultural goods and mining products.

Built in 1893 on the site of the village once ruled by the Ndebele leader Lobengula, Bulawayo is now Zimbabwe's second largest city. Its 620,000 inhabitants live at an elevation of 4,450 feet above sea level. Like Harare, Bulawayo has a pleasant climate, with temperatures ranging from

Courtesy of Earl Scott

Harare, the Zimbabwean capital, is the center of the nation's commercial and governmental activity. The city is located in the northeast on an open plain near the Hunyani River—a fertile area that produces both tobacco and cotton.

17

Laid out in a geometric pattern of right-angled streets, Bulawayo is known for both its many city parks and its importance as a railway and industrial center.

57° F in June to 72° F in October. As the center of Zimbabwe's railway system, Bulawayo has become one of the most important cities in south central Africa for industry and commerce.

Mutare (formerly Umtali), with a population of more than 130,000, is the country's eastern gateway because it lies in the middle of the 200-mile-long Eastern Highlands, which form much of Zimbabwe's border with Mozambique. Situated on the Harare-Beira Railway line, Mutare is a central point for the shipment of locally produced citrus fruits, tea, tobacco, and timber. The city attracts many tourists who enjoy its scenic location in the Vumba Mountains.

This road in the southeastern city of Mutare climbs to 6,000 feet in the Eastern Highlands.

A drawing depicts the ancient fortress at Great Zimbabwe as it was believed to have looked in about A.D. 1400.

2) History and Government

Archaeologists and historians have found evidence of a variety of migrations and short-lived political groupings in Zimbabwe's past. The Great Zimbabwe ruins, for example, demonstrate the existence of a people with a high degree of centralized authority and military organization.

The Earliest People

Many thousands of years ago, groups of organized hunters and gatherers inhabited the territory of present-day Zimbabwe. These groups were related to the Khoisan peoples, whose descendants now live in the modern nations of Botswana, Namibia, and South Africa. In Zimbabwe these hunters and gatherers were gradually conquered by and intermarried with newcomers to the area—the Shona—who spoke one of the Bantu languages. The Shona moved into Zimbabwe about 2,000 years ago. They raised livestock and grew cereal grains using slash-and-burn techniques to clear the land for farming.

The Shona State

By about A.D. 1500 most of present-day Zimbabwe was ruled by Shona hereditary kings known as *Munhumutapa* (sometimes spelled *Mwene Mutapa*). From their walled cities, these monarchs traded gold from their mines with Arab merchants and

Portuguese adventurers, both of whom approached this strong African state from the Indian Ocean. Later, the Portuguese established trading posts within the territory, but they had little success in maintaining these settlements. Their failure was due principally to African resistance, and the Portuguese withdrew from the area in the late seventeenth century.

The Munhumutapa kingdom in the north remained powerful until it was challenged by ethnically related, but southwestern-based, groups of the Changamire or Rozwi kingdom in the late seventeenth century. The aggressive Rozwi peoples conquered the northern Shona peoples and dominated the territory that is now Zimbabwe for over 100 years. With the decline of the Indian Ocean trade in the early nineteenth century, however, the Changamire kingdom weakened. Gradually the unity of the kingdom diminished, causing these various Shona peoples to separate into many small groups.

In the early decades of the 1800s, the Shona began to come into contact with Nguni-speaking groups fleeing the *mfecane* (troubles) in the area that is now South Africa. The troubles stemmed from the aggressive activities of Shaka, the tyrannical ruler of the Zulu people. A powerful and militarily skilled monarch, Shaka—with the aid of his able warriors—eventually established a vast empire. Mzilikazi, one of Shaka's more experienced war leaders, left the king's domain, taking with him a large following. This action provoked Shaka into violent pursuit, and Mzilikazi fled north. Harassed by both Shaka's forces and Afrikaans-speaking white set-

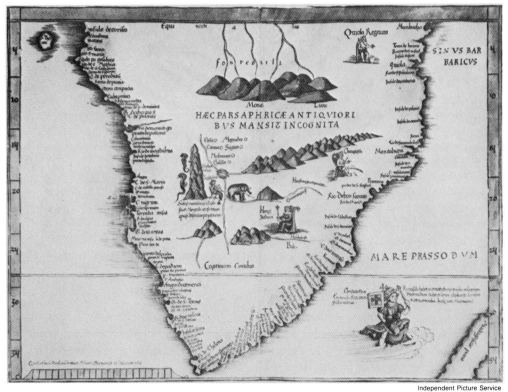

Using maps based on the work of ancient mathematicians, Arab and Portuguese traders traveled to parts of south central Africa—including present-day Zimbabwe—in search of goods and markets.

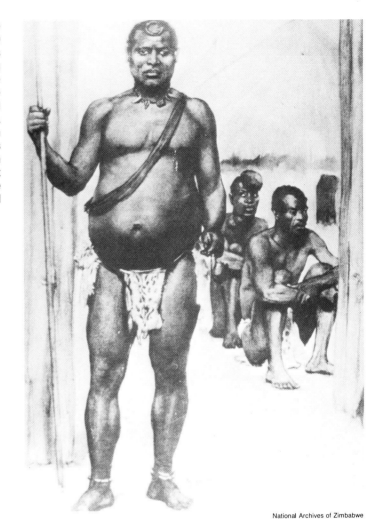

Son of Mzilikazi, Lobengula became king of the Ndebele people in 1870 after two years of conflict about his succession to the throne. Having granted mining concessions to the British, the king began to see the new settlers as a threat and resisted further white territorial expansion. A major battle against the British in 1893 forced Lobengula to yield his capital at Bulawayo. His death in 1894 marked the end of an important period in Zimbabwean history, since British influence rapidly increased from then onward.

tlers, Mzilikazi and his people finally established themselves near the present-day city of Bulawayo in the middle of the nineteenth century. The newcomers to the area came to be called Ndebele, from a local word meaning strangers.

The Missionaries

In 1829, while still on his trek through South Africa, Mzilikazi invited Robert Moffat, a Scottish missionary, to visit him at Mosega. When Mzilikazi eventually settled in Zimbabwe later in the nineteenth century, the friendship between him and the Moffat family continued to flourish.

Robert Moffat's son, John Smith Moffat, started a mission and school at Inyati in 1859 with Mzilikazi's permission. David Livingstone—another Scottish missionary and Robert Moffat's son-in-law—visited Lake Ngami in northwestern Botswana in the late 1840s. During his second visit in 1855, Livingstone saw the Mosuatunya Falls on the Zambezi River and named them Victoria Falls after Queen Victoria of Great Britain.

The missionary efforts of the Moffat family were part of a revived European interest in establishing new colonies in untouched areas of south central Africa. Unfortunately the work of the missionaries also attracted European hunters, who were searching the area for ostrich feathers and ivory.

The Occupation of Zimbabwe

When Mzilikazi died in 1868, he was succeeded by his son Lobengula. At this time much of Europe was scrambling to occupy land in Africa. In 1887 the Transvaalers —Afrikaans-speaking white settlers (sometimes called Boers) living in southern Africa—convinced Lobengula to enter into an alliance, called the Grobler Treaty. Meanwhile, Cecil Rhodes, a rich, enterprising, and forceful British financier, was envisioning the whole of south central Africa

as a huge British colony. Consequently, Rhodes was alarmed at the Transvaaler-Ndebele alliance and convinced the British government to take action.

In February of 1888 John Smith Moffat, by then a British diplomat, told Lobengula that the Grobler Treaty was invalid. Moffat further advised Lobengula to sign a substitute agreement with Great Britain. Under this agreement, the Ndebele king would promise not to have dealings with any other power without Britain's approval. Lobengula signed the treaty but began to mistrust the motives of the British— and with good reason. Rhodes, fired by his grand ambitions, soon came with a force of hired soldiers to take over the land.

Cecil John Rhodes was one of the main promoters of African colonization in the late nineteenth century. His ambitious ideas brought much of southern and eastern Africa, which he straddles in this period cartoon, under British rule.

Independent Picture Service

22

A British delegation—including John Smith Moffat *(third from left)*—**arrived at Lobengula's residence in 1888 to convince the king to ally himself with Great Britain.**

More than any other individual, Cecil Rhodes was responsible for the British occupation and later colonization of Zimbabwe. (Zimbabwe was called Rhodesia—after Rhodes—until 1980.) During his lifetime he dominated the politics of the southern part of the African continent and created a large personal financial empire.

Moffat had succeeded in gaining diplomatic supremacy in the region. This supremacy encouraged Rhodes's agent Charles Rudd to contact Lobengula. Rudd's aim was to secure a monopoly over all mineral and mining rights in the Ndebele kingdom. In exchange for his consent to the monopoly, Lobengula was to receive 100 British pounds (about $500) each month, 1,000 modern guns, and a gunboat. But Rudd misled Lobengula, and the written agreement the king actually signed granted far more to the British than he had consented to verbally.

Rhodes obtained a 25-year royal charter in October 1889 from Queen Victoria of Great Britian to rule the lands of the Shona and the Ndebele. He equipped and paid troops to occupy the Shona territories in 1890 under the umbrella organization of the British South Africa Company. On September 12, 1890, these occupying forces built a fort near some Shona villages presided over by a headman named Harare. The British settlers—frequently termed the Pioneer Column—called their new post Salisbury in honor of Lord Salisbury, the prime minister of Great Britain at the time. Without seeking permission of the local black leaders in Zimbabwe, Rhodes granted fertile farmland and mining claims to his

By 1898 the white settlers of Salisbury (modern Harare) had begun to establish streets and to build more permanent dwellings and businesses than had existed in previous years.

The covered wagons of the British formed a line against the Ndebele warriors in a drawing that depicts the Battle of Egodade. Although Lobengula's troops also carried the traditional weapons depicted here, both sides used guns in the fighting.

troops. Within two years a white population of 3,000 lived in Zimbabwe.

Rhodes recognized the extreme importance of having access to a port that would be nearer to Salisbury than the facilities at Cape Town in South Africa. A treaty that was settled in 1891 between Great Britain and Portugal permitted a railroad to be built from the port of Beira—in the colony of Portuguese East Africa (now Mozambique)—to Salisbury. The treaty also provided for free navigation along the Zambezi River and for the construction of telegraph stations.

African Resistance

The Shona and the Ndebele at first had accepted the white settlers as *vaeni* (friendly strangers). The Africans thought that, like the hunters and the missionaries, the vaeni would stay for only a short time. After the whites established settlements throughout the Shona lands, however, they turned on Lobengula and the Ndebele. In July 1893 one of Lobengula's regiments attacked Shona villagers in the Fort Victoria area because the village had taken some cattle from the Ndebele. This event gave Leander Starr Jameson, a local administrator for Rhodes's company, an excuse to go to war against Lobengula.

Leander Starr Jameson administered much of the territory of present-day Zimbabwe for the British South Africa Company. His success in suppressing the Shona and Ndebele resistance to foreign rule opened the way for British expansion and colonization.

24

With most of his soldiers fighting the Shona in the Zambezi Valley, Lobengula's remaining warriors were no match for the better-armed forces under Jameson. After attempting to surrender, Lobengula fled to the north and died of fever in the early months of 1894.

Three years later both the Ndebele and the Shona revolted against the enslavement and taxes that the settlers forced upon them. Eventually, the white settlers subdued the Shona and the Ndebele because the Europeans had more guns and because they were assisted by African groups who had never accepted the Ndebele presence in Zimbabwe.

Self-Government

When the first period of rule by the British South Africa Company expired in 1914, the British government and the company officers agreed that the charter should be extended for another 10 years. The company's Legislative Council, however, retained the right to ask the British Crown to take over the colonial government at any time during this period. Such a petition was presented in 1919, and a referendum was held in 1922. (Blacks were barred from voting by impossible economic and literacy requirements.) The white voters had to choose between self-government or incorporation into South Africa. The people chose self-government, and on September 12, 1923, the colony of Rhodesia was formally separated from South Africa and annexed to the British Crown. Documents were then issued that made the country a self-governing colony within the British Empire.

The monarchy would be represented by a crown-appointed governor. A unicameral, or one-house, legislature consisting of 30 members would consider laws and regulations, and executive functions would be handled by a prime minister. Except for the addition of a second legislative chamber, this general governmental structure remained in force until Rhodesia's Unilateral Declaration of Independence from Great Britain in 1965.

Representing Southern Rhodesia from 1924 to 1953, the old state flag featured the British Union Jack and a shield carrying a lion and two thistles—images taken from the coat of arms of Cecil Rhodes. The pick and green coloring symbolized the nation's two most important economic activities: mining and farming.

Artwork by Laura Westlund

Federation

In 1951 and 1953 conferences were held to discuss the closer association of Southern Rhodesia (modern Zimbabwe), Northern Rhodesia (modern Zambia), and Nyasaland (modern Malawi), as the three colonies were then called. A federal scheme was drafted and the Federation of Rhodesia and Nyasaland came into existence on September 3, 1953.

The northern territories, however, were strongly opposed to this federation, and for 10 years they demanded the right to separate. In April 1963, therefore, the British government announced that it accepted the right of any of the territories to leave the federation, if they so wished. The federation was accordingly dissolved on December 31, 1963.

Unilateral Declaration of Independence (UDI)

In many ways, Rhodesia had been responsible for its own development since the ar-

Independent Picture Service

Under the white-controlled government of Rhodesia, few blacks were allowed to participate in the political process. Revised constitutions in the 1960s changed this imbalance to some degree. Here, African members of the national legislature, called the House of Assembly, enter the chamber in the 1970s.

Independent Picture Service

Surrounded by his cabinet ministers, Ian Douglas Smith signed the proclamation that declared Rhodesia's independence from Great Britain on November 11, 1965.

26

Independent Picture Service

Critics of the Smith government asserted that Rhodesia's policies of racial separateness favored the white minority. Schools, for example, were segregated, and facilities for black children *(above)* were not equal in quality to the educational services available to white Rhodesian students *(below)*.

rival of Rhodes in 1890. Formally, it had governed itself since 1923, although certain types of legislation required the approval of the British government. In 1961 white Rhodesian voters endorsed a new constitution. It widened the voting privilege to include some black Rhodesians and increased the legislative powers of the Rhodesian government.

On November 11, 1965, the government of Rhodesia made a Unilateral Declaration of Independence (UDI) from Great Britain, which gave Rhodesia complete authority over its own affairs. Asked to decide what kind of independent government they wanted, 81 percent of the white voters opted for a republic. A new constitution reflecting the new status was drawn up and passed by the Rhodesian Parliament in early 1969. On March 2, 1970, Rhodesia officially became a republic, although Great Britain, the United Nations, and the black majority in Rhodesia did not recognize the event.

Independent Picture Service

27

Sanctions

After Rhodesia's declaration of independence, the United Nations—as well as countries in Africa and the Western world—imposed sanctions against the new republic that forbade any trade or diplomatic relations with Rhodesia. The sanctions arose from the view that Rhodesia discriminated against its black population on political, social, and economic levels.

The white Rhodesians denied this assertion, claiming that blacks in white-controlled Rhodesia were better off than they would be in most republics governed by blacks. White Rhodesians went on to point out that the black Rhodesians had been provided with homes, schools, hospitals, churches, libraries, and recreational facilities. Whites also claimed that blacks had the opportunities to advance as far as their own abilities and training would allow.

The government of Rhodesia did not want to lose either Great Britain's friendship or its trade. The sanctions put both countries at a disadvantage. In order to achieve a settlement, Britain sent a peace commission to Rhodesia in 1972 to find out how black Rhodesians felt about the situation. Their reactions convinced Britain that the blacks were not at all satisfied with the political arrangement in Rhodesia.

Black opposition in Rhodesia was organized under the leadership of Joshua Nkomo (left) **and Robert Mugabe** (right).

A mural at Heroes Acres in Harare depicts the independence struggle – including the seven-year civil war – that resulted in the establishment of the Republic of Zimbabwe.

Black Opposition Organizes

Since the black population of Zimbabwe was never consulted by the white minority in the 1965 declaration of Rhodesian independence, the blacks did not accept the resulting new government. Leaders among the black population responded to this unresolved situation by organizing into political groups. On December 18, 1961, the Zimbabwe African People's Union (ZAPU) was founded with Joshua Nkomo as president and Robert Mugabe as secretary for publicity. The purpose of their organization was to work for rule by the majority. The colonial government outlawed ZAPU in September 1962, and Nkomo and Mugabe left the country. After a disagreement arose between them, Mugabe and Nkomo established two separate organizations to fight minority rule.

By April 1966 the exiled Zimbabwe African National Union (ZANU), headed by Robert Mugabe, was sending trained guerrilla fighters back into Rhodesia from Zambia. In July 1967 Nkomo's ZAPU forces fought Rhodesian troops near Hwange.

Civil War

By 1972 a full-scale civil war was in progress in Rhodesia. As the fighting continued, the guerrilla army gained support from the majority of the black population and sharpened its ability to conduct a hit-and-run guerrilla offensive. The government, under Rhodesian prime minister Ian Douglas Smith, responded by forcing Zimbabweans into isolated camps to prevent the uncommitted local populations from supporting the rebels. This action succeeded only in increasing the resistance of the majority of black Zimbabweans to the established white government.

In December 1974 ZAPU, ZANU, and some other nationalist parties met in Lusaka, Zambia, and attempted to form a united political front under Bishop Abel Muzorewa. In September 1975 Robert Mugabe, leader of ZANU, organized a common effort by the military wings of both ZANU and ZAPU called the Zimbabwe People's Army. This united effort lasted only until the end of 1976. From then on the majority of the fighting was carried on by the ZANU military wing, known as the Zimbabwe African National Liberation Army.

In retaliation, Rhodesian forces bombed civilian refugee camps in Mozambique, Zambia, Botswana, and Angola, killing thousands of people. By late 1975—despite harsh reprisals, torture of civilians, and military-imposed law throughout most of the country—the Zimbabwean guerrillas were defeating the forces of the Rhodesian government. Estimates indicate that 20,000 Zimbabweans—mostly guerrilla fighters—died in the conflict.

Zimbabwean Independence

On March 3, 1978, in a last attempt to retain minority power over Rhodesian affairs, Ian Douglas Smith convinced Bishop Muzorewa and some other black leaders to join his government in an effort to end the violence. This arrangement—rejected by all of the guerrilla leaders—lasted a little over a year. After the breakdown of the coalition government, meetings were proposed in London to consider how to resolve the conflict.

From September 10 to December 21, 1979, the Patriotic Front (PF)—led jointly by Robert Mugabe and Joshua Nkomo with delegates from both ZANU and ZAPU—met at Lancaster House in London with Bishop Muzorewa, Smith, and others in a constitutional conference. For over two months the delegates ironed out a cease-fire, wrote a new constitution, and made arrangements for governing the country in the interim period between the end of the civil war and the establishment of the Republic of Zimbabwe.

From December 1979 to April 17, 1980, Zimbabwe was again ruled as the British colony of Southern Rhodesia (called Zimbabwe-Rhodesia). At midnight on April 17 the former colony began its history as an independent republic.

Courtesy of Earl Scott

A trio of guerrilla fighters is commemorated in a statue in Harare.

Robert Mugabe was instrumental in the successful drive to end minority rule in Zimbabwe. Between 1980 and 1987, Mugabe served as Zimbabwe's prime minister. Since 1987—when Mugabe's ZANU-PF party merged with Nkomo's ZAPU party—Mugabe has headed a one-party state as executive president.

The Postindependence Era

After the establishment of the Republic of Zimbabwe, the new government—with Robert Mugabe as prime minister—aimed to heal the divisions created by the civil war. Ian Smith, for example, retained his parliamentary seat and freely debated his views in the legislature. In addition, Joshua Nkomo—Mugabe's long-time rival—became a member of the new cabinet.

This process of cooperation did not last long, however. Nkomo was dismissed from the cabinet in 1982 after he was accused of supporting antigovernment rebels, and Smith's Republican Front party split into factions. Violence overshadowed the 1985 elections—Zimbabwe's first general elections since independence. Voters gave Mugabe's ZANU-PF party a majority of seats, and he won another five-year term as prime minister.

In the mid-1980s fighting erupted between the Ndebele people—a minority ethnic group that supported ZAPU, Nkomo's opposition party—and the majority Shona, who backed ZANU-PF. In 1985 Nkomo began talks with Mugabe to heal the division between these two groups. The outcome of their discussions was a 1987 agreement to merge Nkomo's ZAPU party with the dominant ZANU-PF party. This move effectively made Zimbabwe a one-party state.

Under the 1987 agreement, Mugabe broadened his powers as head of the government. He became Zimbabwe's first executive president—a position that combines the posts of prime minister and president. He also was named president and first secretary of ZANU-PF. Appointed as one of three high-ranking ministers, Nkomo directed several important ministries that were involved with development in rural areas. In 1990 he was appointed vice president, a post he held through the mid-1990s.

31

In the late 1980s, international human rights organizations accused Mugabe's government of abusing prisoners and of detaining dissenters. Pressure from these organizations lessened in 1990 when the government lifted a 25-year state of emergency. This policy had permitted officials to hold people as prisoners without trial. All political detainees were released when the state of emergency expired.

In 1996 Mugabe won a third term as president. Legislative elections had confirmed the overwhelming majority of the ZANU-PF party, which holds 148 of the 150 seats in the House of Assembly. But opposition groups, who accused the government of manipulating the vote, boycotted the elections. Dissidents within Zimbabwe and exiles in neighboring Mozambique still protest the one-party rule of ZANU-PF.

Governmental Structure

The 1987 agreement between Mugabe and Nkomo brought about a major change in

Courtesy of John H. Peck

Some of Zimbabwe's local government is still in the hands of traditional ethnic leaders, or chiefs. Here, Chief Murape and his wife stand next to the new well at their farm near Domboshawu, north of Harare.

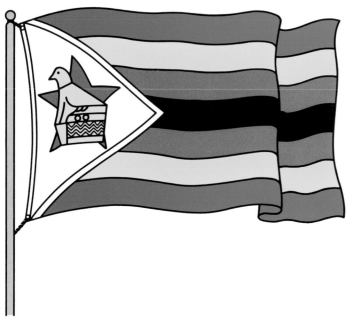

Artwork by Laura Westlund

A new national flag came into use after Zimbabwean independence was achieved in 1980. The green stripes signify the land and its resources; yellow is for the country's wealth. The color red symbolizes the blood shed in the struggle for self-rule, and black represents the ethnic majority of the population. The Zimbabwe bird, found among the ruins of Great Zimbabwe, has become the nation's symbol, reminding the people of their past.

The High Court of Zimbabwe, located in Harare, is presided over by a chief justice who is appointed by the executive president.

the structure of Zimbabwe's government. Formerly a parliamentary democracy—with a head of government (the prime minister) and a head of state (the president)—Zimbabwe now combines the jobs of prime minister and president into the office of executive president.

The executive president is elected to a six-year term by a vote in the legislature. These votes are determined by a popular vote. The executive president names vice presidents, cabinet ministers, and members of the judicial branch. The executive president can also veto legislation passed by Parliament.

Zimbabwe has a one-house legislature known as the House of Assembly. Members of the House of Assembly are elected for six-year terms. Of the 150 legislators, 120 are elected by a popular vote, 10 hold seats as tribal chiefs, 12 are appointed by the Zimbabwean president, and 8 hold seats as provincial governors. A two-thirds majority in the House of Assembly is necessary to make changes in the constitution. A Declaration of Rights guarantees fundamental rights and freedoms of all Zimbabwean citizens.

In August 1987, the legislature voted to end the practice of reserving 30 parliamentary seats for whites. This arrangement for whites had been agreed to in 1980 to guarantee white representation in Zimbabwe's new black-majority government. White Zimbabwean citizens are still eligible to run for any public office and to vote in all elections.

Bills passed by the House of Assembly are presented to the executive president. If the executive president accepts the bill, it becomes a law that governs the country. A presidential veto of a piece of legislation can be overridden if two-thirds of the members of the legislature vote to support the bill.

The country's chief justice and at least two other justices preside over the Zimbabwean Supreme Court. This court enforces the Declaration of Rights and serves as the final court of appeal. The chief justice also heads the High Court, which holds authority over all of the country's trials. Regional and magistrate courts hear criminal cases. Local courts decide civil and minor criminal cases.

For administrative purposes, Zimbabwe is divided into eight provinces. A governor, whom the executive president appoints, administers each province with the help of local ministries.

In Harare, high school students from St. John's College *(in green and white uniforms)* and from Eaglesville College play a spirited game of rugby.

3) The People

Immediately after independence, the situation in Zimbabwe looked fairly optimistic. Educational and rural health facilities expanded rapidly, and black Zimbabweans entered the civil service in large numbers. The new government, helped by international financial aid, purchased lands owned by white farmers and assisted black Zimbabweans in resettling them. Some Zimbabweans, who believed in the struggle for independence, have been rather disappointed at the slow pace of social progress since the new government came to power. Nevertheless, Zimbabwe has been able to offer both its black and its white citizens relatively peaceful solutions to the conflicts that exist between them.

Ethnic Composition

Most of Zimbabwe's 11.5 million people are blacks of the Shona and Ndebele groups, who are related to the Bantu-speaking populations of neighboring countries. The Shona people make up about 80 percent of the population and historically have lived in the country longer than other groups. The Ndebele represent about 19 percent of the population and, until recently, were centered in the area around Bulawayo, where they had settled upon their arrival from South Africa in the nineteenth century.

About 100,000 Zimbabweans are white, 10,000 are Asian, and more than 20,000 are of mixed origins. The black population has

Courtesy of Tim Krieger

About three-quarters of Zimbabwe's black population live in rural areas, many of which are distinguished by small clusters of traditional, straw-covered dwellings.

Photo by Amandus Schneider

In contrast to the countryside, however, urban centers like Harare feature busy streets and tall skyscrapers. Most of Zimbabwe's white population live in the cities.

A rural woman explains her techniques for cooking over an open, wood-fueled fire. Household services, such as electricity and plumbing, have yet to reach many Zimbabwean villages.

an annual growth rate of 3.1 percent, while the other groups are growing at a much slower rate. More than 75 percent of the whites are urban dwellers. Roughly the same percentage of blacks live in rural areas. Approximately 750,000 rural people sought refuge in the cities during the struggle for independence, but most of them have returned to the countryside. Similarly, whites—mostly urban professionals, who fled the country at an average rate of 1,400 a month just after independence—have begun to return to Zimbabwe.

More than half of the white citizens—who are primarily of British origin—are relative newcomers to Zimbabwe, arriving after World War II. Afrikaners from South Africa and European minorities also are present, including some people of Portuguese origin from Mozambique. English, the official language of Zimbabwe, is spoken by the white population and understood—if not always used—by more than half of the black citizens.

Basket weaving produces both attractive artworks and useful articles for the home. Here, a village craftswoman works on a new piece, with an example of her skill at her side.

36

With their babies slung from their backs, these rural women pound corn into flour with two long mallets.

Practical Handicrafts

The rural population of Zimbabwe continues to make a wide variety of articles for daily use. Carved wooden headrests, ornamented knives and gourds, baskets containing panels of carved wood, musical instruments, and a wide variety of earthenware pots are made throughout the countryside. The most striking common feature of these objects is their rich, geometric decoration.

As elsewhere in Africa, many Zimbabwean children make their own toys using clay or soft wire. For example, they bend the wire to make detailed models of trucks, cars, airplanes, and bicycles. These intricately designed toys often have parts that move as the model is steered along the road by a long handle.

Roof thatching—an even more practical art form—is still very common in the countryside. The grass for the roof is carefully chosen for its length. Women bundle and comb the selected grasses, and men are the thatchers. They arrange the bundles on a roof, beginning at the eaves and building toward the center. The thatchers attach the grass to the roof by repeatedly winding a coarse string around the bundle onto the frame of the dwelling until the bundle is

Musical instruments, such as drums, are commonly made by hand.

Zimbabwean children often design and produce their own toys. Fashioned of soft wire, this small truck is steered by a long handle.

Courtesy of Tom O'Toole

Thatchers carefully arrange bundles of dried grass on a roof and secure them with durable string.

When finished, a professionally thatched roof is good protection from the effects of rain and sun.

Courtesy of John H. Peck

39

securely tied. Layer is placed upon layer until only a small opening remains at the top, over which a cap of thatch is fastened.

Wood Carving and Sculpture

Artists continue to make wooden masks according to age-old designs. The most common mask is oval and often has two horns sticking out from a heavily grooved forehead. Narrow slits represent the eyes, and the broad, sharp nose has lines cut into it. Similar lines stretch across the cheekbones, and the mouth is open, with pursed lips. Dancers in religious ceremonies once used masks made of wood, straw, and other materials to enhance the rituals.

At a number of mission-operated schools, wood-carvers have blended this traditional art form with Western themes. For example, Shona sculpture—perhaps the most significant development in Zimbabwean art—began in the workshop of Harare's National Gallery during the 1960s. Since then, these stone sculptures have achieved international recognition and are eagerly sought by art collectors.

Literature and Drama

The people of Zimbabwe have a rich story-telling tradition that expresses itself in legends, epic poems, praise-songs, and ballads that have been handed down orally from generation to generation. In addition to traditional oral literature, there is a flourishing market for published works in English and in the Ndebele and Shona languages. Commercial firms and the government-backed Literature Bureau produce a wide range of publications. These materials include technical and educational books, drama, poetry, nonfiction, novels, and children's literature. Over 150 authors writing in the Shona and Ndebele languages have produced a wealth of novels and short stories. Some of these authors also write outstanding verse in English.

Courtesy of Tim Krieger

This wood-carver has produced an artwork that tells the story of Nyaminyami, a god of the Zambezi River who, according to tradition, was separated from his wife when the Kariba Dam was built.

Pre-independence authors, such as Doris Lessing in *The Grass Is Singing*, have described the world of the white settlers in Zimbabwe. The black experience, on the other hand, is the focus of Dambudzo Marechera's *The House of Hunger*, Charles L. Mungoshi's *Waiting for the Rain*, and Stanlake Samkange's *On Trial for My Country* and *The Year of the Uprising.*

About 30 Zimbabwean theater groups present regular productions in a network of expertly designed theaters throughout the country. The National Theatre Organization, which is deeply involved in nurturing Zimbabwean playwrights and in helping to establish theater workshops, coordinates dramatic activity throughout the country.

Music and Dance

Music is a constant presence in Zimbabwe. When music is for dancing, its style is flamboyant, and the *manyawi* (the spirit of expression and excitement) develops the pace of the tune. If, however, the music is for a solemn occasion, musicians hold back the tempo to create a serious mood. Many lyrics simply express everyday events.

A completely self-taught artist, Joshua Mariga puts the finishing touches on a soapstone figure at his workshop in Inyanga.

Zimbabweans have a long-lived tradition of storytelling that finds an outlet here at a village gathering of local leaders.

A vividly masked dancer illustrates Zimbabwe's strong ties to its cultural past.

For example, a babysitter sings a nurse's song to a baby when its mother is working in the fields, or a midwife chants a presentation song when she gives a newborn baby to its father.

The most important musical instrument in Zimbabwe is the drum. Drums are made in a number of sizes to provide a variety of tones and pitches and are usually carved from solid blocks of wood with designs cut or burnt into them.

Marimbas are also very popular instruments. Like the xylophone, a marimba is made of strips of wood that vary in length, which are attached to a soundboard. Musicians strike the strips with wooden hammers to produce the melody. Marimbas can vary considerably in size, which affects their pitch, and a group of these instruments may be played together as a band. The handheld *mbira* works on a similar principle but is smaller. The sound is produced from iron rods fixed to a wooden soundboard. These rods are plucked with the thumb or forefinger to provide a melody.

In much of Zimbabwe's music, drums are the most important instrument and provide a dramatic background to dances.

Most Zimbabwean dances combine graceful and energetic movements *(above)* with an important message. Two dancers *(below)* act out a musical scenario of the colonial takeover of Zimbabwe, when one group of people physically controlled the actions of another.

In Zimbabwe music is almost always accompanied by dancing as a means of self-expression. Dancing is a vital part of all social gatherings, including parties, weddings, political meetings, and receptions for visiting officials. Even religious occasions, such as funerals, include dancing as part of the rituals.

The Church of Santa Barbara in Kariba serves Zimbabwe's Christian community.

Religion

More than 25 percent of the people of Zimbabwe are members of Christian churches. Given the major contribution of Christian missions to education and health care for black Zimbabweans from the 1890s onward, it is not surprising that most of Zimbabwe's present leaders have Christian backgrounds.

Since independence, however, the growth of Christianity has slowed to a great extent. About one-half of Zimbabwe's people are members of independent African churches that, to various degrees, combine elements of local religious practices with Christian rituals. Traditional religions, which focus on ancestral spirits and their effects on the living, continue to be widely practiced in rural areas.

Some educational courses are aimed at practical concerns. These women are learning basic cooking skills at a vocational school.

Education

Until about 1950, Christian missionaries provided most formal education. Of the present adult population, over 41 percent have had no formal schooling.

According to the Zimbabwean constitution, free primary education is required for all the nation's children. By the mid-1990s, the country had built 4,500 primary and 1,500 secondary schools. Many local communities have built new schools but must wait for qualified teachers. The central government pays the salaries of the primary school teachers, but the schools themselves are owned and run by local councils, missions, business firms, and private individuals.

The student union at the University of Zimbabwe in Harare is a focus of gatherings and academic activity on the campus.

Gideon Mhlanga, the first black Rhodesian to earn a college degree and then to teach in his country, stands in front of the Gazaland Secondary School, which he helped to establish in the late 1960s.

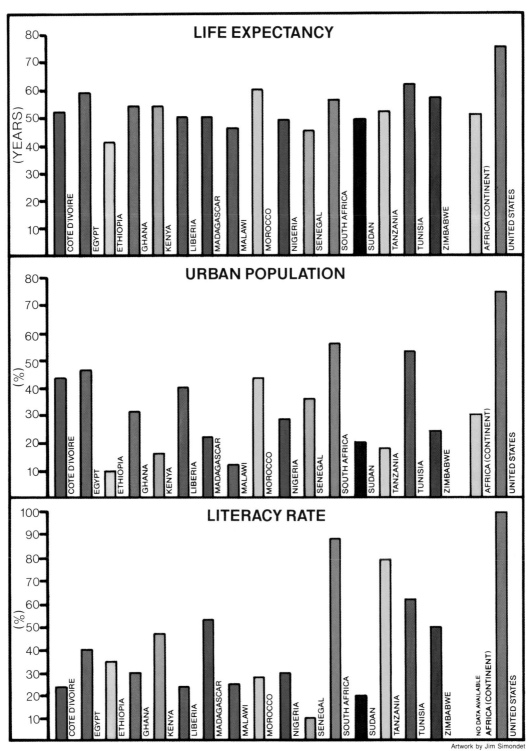

LIFE EXPECTANCY

(YEARS)

- COTE D'IVOIRE
- EGYPT
- ETHIOPIA
- GHANA
- KENYA
- LIBERIA
- MADAGASCAR
- MALAWI
- MOROCCO
- NIGERIA
- SENEGAL
- SOUTH AFRICA
- SUDAN
- TANZANIA
- TUNISIA
- ZIMBABWE
- AFRICA (CONTINENT)
- UNITED STATES

URBAN POPULATION

(%)

- COTE D'IVOIRE
- EGYPT
- ETHIOPIA
- GHANA
- KENYA
- LIBERIA
- MADAGASCAR
- MALAWI
- MOROCCO
- NIGERIA
- SENEGAL
- SOUTH AFRICA
- SUDAN
- TANZANIA
- TUNISIA
- ZIMBABWE
- AFRICA (CONTINENT)
- UNITED STATES

LITERACY RATE

(%)

- COTE D'IVOIRE
- EGYPT
- ETHIOPIA
- GHANA
- KENYA
- LIBERIA
- MADAGASCAR
- MALAWI
- MOROCCO
- NIGERIA
- SENEGAL
- SOUTH AFRICA
- SUDAN
- TANZANIA
- TUNISIA
- ZIMBABWE
- NO DATA AVAILABLE AFRICA (CONTINENT)
- UNITED STATES

Artwork by Jim Simondet

The three factors depicted in this graph suggest differences in the quality of life among 16 African nations. Averages for the United States and the entire continent of Africa are included for comparison. (Data taken from "1987 World Population Data Sheet" and *PC-Globe.*)

The Zimbabwean government hopes to be able to provide secondary schooling for all those who seek it. The rapid program of school building allowed the number of secondary-school students to increase by 10 times between 1980 and 1995. About 90 percent of all school-aged children are now enrolled, and Zimbabwe's literacy rate has reached 80 percent.

The University of Zimbabwe, founded in 1955, serves the higher educational needs of the country. Approximately 5,000 students are enrolled in classes that focus on agriculture, the arts, commerce, law, education, engineering, and medicine. The University of Science and Technology enrolls students at Bulawayo. Zimbabwe also has two private universities, as well as teacher-training, agricultural, and technical colleges.

Health

Programs enacted by the government aim to meet Zimbabwe's basic health-care needs. Emphasis in these programs is on the prevention of disease and the promotion of good health habits. The World Health Organization coordinates research and testing of AIDS (acquired immune deficiency syndrome) in Africa. More than 7,411 cases of this epidemic disease have been documented in Zimbabwe – mostly in Harare and other urban centers.

In 1995 Zimbabwe's infant mortality rate stood at 53 deaths for each 1,000 live births. The life expectancy figure was 62 years. Both of these rates are better in Zimbabwe than they are in most of Africa. Compared to industrialized nations, however, the figures reveal that much still needs to be done to improve health standards.

Plans have been made to build and expand rural hospitals and clinics so that no one will have to walk more than about five miles to reach a medical facility. Eighteen training hospitals have been built to cope with the increased demand for nurses and

Nganga, or local healers, use a variety of natural products, such as herbs and plants, to address the health needs of Zimbabweans who seek their help.

medical assistants, and the University of Zimbabwe is attempting to graduate enough doctors to fill the country's growing demand. The rural and district councils are responsible for clinics in their areas, and many missions have clinics or hospitals that serve the rural population. Urban centers have fairly adequate hospital facilities to care for city dwellers and for patients in need of special attention who have been sent from rural districts.

Medical students, student nurses, and midwives are assigned to rural villages as part of their training experience. These trainees assist health workers who are already established in the villages. Provincial health workers and some voluntary organizations conduct educational programs on health and nutrition. By law, medical care in Zimbabwe is free to anyone earning less than $150 per month.

Nganga (local healers) are officially recognized figures in the health services of Zimbabwe. Some Nganga use herbs for their treatment of patients, while others rely on their knowledge of local customs and beliefs to cure or to prevent illness. Most Nganga belong to the national association for Nganga, called the Zimbabwe National Traditional Healers Association (ZINATHA).

Zimbabwean farmers produce surplus corn in years of good weather. Milled sacks of the crop are stacked for distribution to domestic markets.

4) The Economy

Zimbabwe has three natural, wealth-producing resources—farmland, mines, and wild animals in settings of great beauty. For many years, agriculture was the leading factor in the economy, but the industrial mining sector has grown rapidly. Furthermore, the preservation of animals and the country's natural beauty have begun to generate substantial revenues from the tourist industry.

Agriculture

Despite Zimbabwe's variety of farming products, most agricultural cultivation is for personal consumption. Farmers supplement their incomes by small sales of livestock or by migrant farm work. Tobacco growing still earns the most revenue, but cultivation of corn, wheat, and sugar cane now outpaces tobacco in volume. Other crops grown in profitable quantities are sorghum (a cereal grain), rice, barley, cotton, coffee, peanuts, soybeans, sunflowers, tea, beans, and potatoes. A serious drought in 1992 and 1993 forced the country to import much of its food.

Several irrigation projects and the adoption of modern farming techniques have increased Zimbabwe's crop yields. Zimbabwean farmers produce surplus corn in good years, generate high export earnings from cotton sales, and grow enough sorghum to supply all of the malt (soaked grain) for Zimbabwe's beer-brewing industry. Increased irrigation and varieties

These workers are bagging a recently picked cotton crop. Production of cotton has increased since the drought of 1992.

Traditionally, tobacco has been Zimbabwe's main export product. Laborers *(left)* tie huge tobacco leaves together to dry in the shade.

A worker on a tea estate in northeastern Zimbabwe prunes tea plants with a sickle, or curved knife.

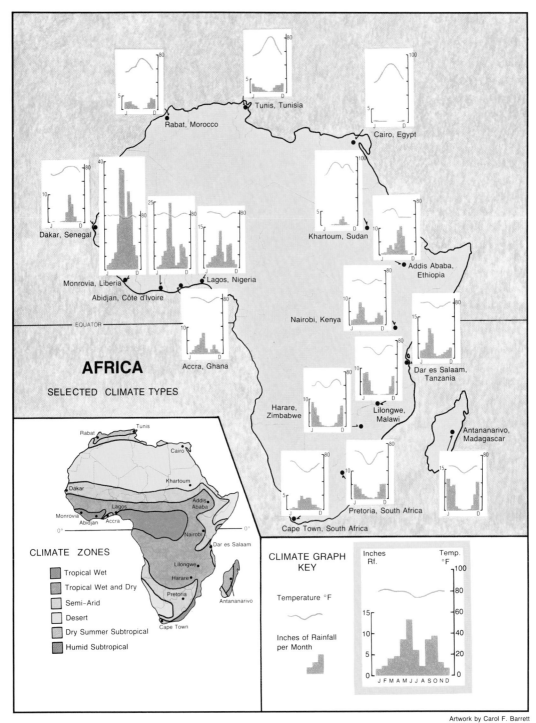

AFRICA

SELECTED CLIMATE TYPES

Rabat, Morocco
Tunis, Tunisia
Cairo, Egypt
Dakar, Senegal
Khartoum, Sudan
Addis Ababa, Ethiopia
Monrovia, Liberia
Abidjan, Côte d'Ivoire
Lagos, Nigeria
Nairobi, Kenya
Accra, Ghana
Dar es Salaam, Tanzania
Harare, Zimbabwe
Lilongwe, Malawi
Antananarivo, Madagascar
Pretoria, South Africa
Cape Town, South Africa

EQUATOR

CLIMATE ZONES

Rabat
Tunis
Cairo
Khartoum
Dakar
Addis Ababa
Lagos
Monrovia
Abidjan   Accra
Nairobi
Dar es Salaam
Lilongwe
Harare
Pretoria
Antananarivo
Cape Town

☐ Tropical Wet
☐ Tropical Wet and Dry
☐ Semi–Arid
☐ Desert
☐ Dry Summer Subtropical
☐ Humid Subtropical

CLIMATE GRAPH KEY

Inches
Rf.

Temp.
°F

Temperature °F

Inches of Rainfall
per Month

J F M A M J J A S O N D

Artwork by Carol F. Barrett

These climate graphs show the monthly change in the average rainfall received and in the average temperature from January to December for the capital cities of 16 African nations. On the graph for Harare, Zimbabwe, "winter" occurs in June, July, and August because the capital is in the Southern Hemisphere. A marked contrast also exists between dry "winter" and wet "summer," when Harare receives nearly all of its 34 inches of average annual rainfall. (Data taken from *World-Climates* by Willy Rudloff, Stuttgart, 1981.)

Once harvested, coffee beans must be turned frequently to ensure that they dry evenly.

of wheat that are better-suited to Zimbabwean weather conditions have made the country nearly self-sufficient in its wheat production. Large amounts of tobacco and coffee are exported, and vegetables—especially potatoes—are marketed to other African countries.

Livestock accounts for roughly 25 to 30 percent of Zimbabwe's agricultural output. The country's cattle population amounts to five million head, more than half of which graze on communal pastureland. The annual production of beef in the early 1990s nearly supplied the domestic needs of Zimbabwe. The potential for exporting some of Zimbabwe's livestock to the European Union (EU) has further strengthened the animal husbandry sector of the economy.

Sheared sheep graze on lands in southern Zimbabwe that belong to a European ranch owner.

Land Resettlement

Zimbabwe's agricultural expansion has been greatly aided by the government. The Agricultural and Rural Development Authority (ARDA) introduces new schemes for agricultural growth and improvement in the countryside. The ARDA's most difficult task has been to oversee the resettlement of thousands of black Zimbabweans who either were displaced by the civil war or whose ancestors were forced out when their lands were granted to British colonists.

The resettlement schemes follow three basic patterns. In the first type, village settlements are established with individual plots of cropland and common grazing. The second pattern features settlements that have communal living quarters and use cooperative farming techniques. The third kind of resettlement involves individually owned parcels of farmland that are part of a central estate operated by the ARDA.

Courtesy of Tim Krieger

On a piece of resettled agricultural land, **Liberty Mhlanga** *(right),* **general manager of the ARDA, inspects a fine grade of tea with the manager of the plant.**

Courtesy of Earl Scott

Under white-controlled governments, townships *(above)* and communal lands were set aside for the resettlement of blacks, whose farms and established communities were given to British immigrants. The lands assigned to the blacks were less fertile and were poorly furnished—if at all—with roads, schools, and health services.

The Katiyo Tea Estates were once part of the Tribal Trust Lands Development Corporation, which divided land ownership into racially segregated areas. In the mid-twentieth century, Rhodesia's 6 million Africans were allocated 44 million acres of land in overcrowded areas, where soil erosion was a serious problem. In contrast, 250,000 white Rhodesians shared an additional 44 million acres of land, principally located in the fertile High Veld. The land resettlement schemes now in progress in Zimbabwe have changed the ownership and usage of the Katiyo Estates to benefit all the nation's peoples.

Forestry

Forests in northwestern Zimbabwe yield teakwood, which is used as support timber in the mines and as crossbars on railway tracks. More than 124,000 acres of pine plantations were planted in the eastern districts under the colonial administration, and the present government's goal is

On plantations in the Eastern Highlands, wattle trees are harvested for their bark—a source of tannin. This substance is used to make ink, dyes, and medicine.

to have 300,000 acres planted by the end of the twentieth century. About 69,000 acres of eucalyptus plantations exist throughout the country. The forest industry has made little progress, however, since the need for domestic firewood has caused whole areas of precious timber to be cut down for fuel.

Manufacturing

The industrial sector of the Zimbabwean economy—one of the most highly developed in Africa—is the greatest contributor to the turnover of money in the country. A variety of industries supplies goods for everyday domestic needs, and surplus manufactured goods flow through Zimbabwe's growing export market. Specialized items, however, such as medical instruments and electronic equipment, continue to be imported. The demand for these goods within the country has not been great enough to make setting up factories to produce them a profitable idea.

In some ways the economic sanctions that were imposed on the Rhodesian government in the 1970s have proven beneficial to independent Zimbabwe. Forced to become economically and industrially self-reliant, the independent Rhodesian regime —with the help of black labor and of raw materials supplied by South Africa—made great strides in manufacturing import substitutes during the 1970s.

Zimbabwe produces a far greater percentage of its consumer goods than do African countries of comparable size. Cement, fertilizers, and most foodstuffs—including cooking oils, canned goods, and beer—are processed locally. Domestic markets for glass, paper, rubber products, and textiles are all satisfied by goods made in Zimbabwean factories.

Zimbabwe's abundance and variety of raw materials, its stable economy, and its cheap fuel and water supplies combine to encourage industrial development. In addition, taxes are low, there is a large work

Courtesy of John H. Peck

Modern equipment at the Katiyo Tea Estates helped to produce a blend that received the highest bid of any tea on the London Tea Market in 1984.

Courtesy of Tim Krieger

A mahogany tree dwarfs an onlooker at the **Mount Selinda** rain-forest in the Eastern Highlands.

54

Women wrap and pack some of Zimbabwe's fruit harvest for shipment to foreign and domestic markets.

The Inyanga Trout Farm, located in eastern Zimbabwe, raises fish for sale to restaurants in urban centers.

These buildings at an industrial site in Harare are used for tobacco processing and storage.

A factory on the outskirts of the capital produces plastic bags from polyethylene, a resin derived from petroleum.

Zimbabwe's growing manufacturing strength is represented by this plant that produces sulfuric acid, which is used as an industrial drying agent.

force available, and transportation and financial services are comprehensive as well as efficient.

Mining

In the early colonial days, southern Africa's mineral wealth lured Europeans and North Americans to Zimbabwe. Although no bottomless gold mines were ever found, the country has been a steady producer of this precious metal since colonial times. Almost 600,000 ounces of fine gold were produced in Zimbabwe in 1991.

The mining industry also furnishes 34 different minerals and metals. Chromite, asbestos, coal, copper, gold, iron ore, limestone, lithium, phosphate rock, and tin are Zimbabwe's chief mining resources. The country's deposits of chromite—from which chrome is made—are among the largest in the world, and its lithium industry is a major global supplier to chemical, plastics, and atomic energy enterprises.

Zimbabwe's coal-mining business is well established at Hwange, where a mining complex was built in 1903. Zimbabwe is one of the few African countries in which both essential minerals and electrical power are available in large quantities. Consequently, both copper and tin mining enjoy consistent growth.

International mining companies are searching for large deposits of low-grade gold ore believed to be present in Zimbabwe. Increased world prices for gold may enable Zimbabwe to reopen mines that had previously been closed because the gold price had been too low to make the mines profitable.

Transportation

Compared to most other African nations, Zimbabwe's rail, land, and air transportation facilities are very well established. Even though they are in need of considerable rehabilitation and strengthening, these networks remain generally adequate for the commercial sectors of the Zimbabwean economy. Since independence, however, much emphasis has been given to the construction of roads to serve rural areas, which were neglected under the white-controlled government.

Rail lines cover most of the country except for the region south of Lake Kariba. The government-owned National Railway of Zimbabwe connects with the South African rail system. The Zimbabwean line is generally well maintained and has connections to the Mozambique ports of Maputo and Beira.

About 20 percent of the roads in Zimbabwe are maintained by the national government. These important arteries link the country's principal towns, commercial farming regions, recreational and tourist

Zimbabwe has a well-developed road network, which is especially important in a landlocked country. The quality of secondary routes (right) depends on the amount of attention and local money spent on their maintenance.

Courtesy of Phil Porter

Courtesy of John H. Peck

On all-weather highways, buses are able to provide year-round transportation services.

areas, main border points, and major zones of economic development. Local councils —both in rural and urban areas—are responsible for the upkeep of the vast majority of roads. These secondary paths can be gravel thoroughfares or little more than dirt tracks, depending on the attention given to them and on the money available for their upkeep.

Air Zimbabwe, the national airline, has a monopoly on the well-traveled internal routes, while private companies provide services to smaller communities. Several international and regional airlines fly into Harare, Bulawayo, and Victoria Falls. Air Zimbabwe also has international flights to Europe and many neighboring African countries.

In rural areas, where roads are poor and vehicles are scarce, walking is still a common way of getting from one place to another.

Courtesy of Tim Krieger

58

Tourism

Zimbabwe's tourist receipts in the mid-1990s—about $100 million annually—boosted tourism to one of the major industries in the economy. Visitors to Zimbabwe enjoy the moderate climate, the beautiful scenery, and the chance to see a wide variety of animals in the natural settings of the country's many national parks.

Victoria Falls—a spectacular natural attraction—and Lake Kariba contribute to the thriving tourist trade. The lake area offers exciting fishing expeditions throughout the year, where anglers can try their luck at catching tiger fish, bream, barbel, and eel. Great Zimbabwe and Mount Inyangani draw many visitors yearly, and the famous Balancing Rocks at Epworth, located near prehistoric cave paintings, attract Zimbabweans and foreigners alike.

Courtesy of Tim Krieger

The Balancing Rocks at Epworth, on the eastern outskirts of Harare, are a popular tourist attraction.

Courtesy of Tim Krieger

Zebras and impalas graze in Mana Pools National Park, a much-visited spot in northern Zimbabwe along the Zambezi River.

59

Tourism offers Zimbabweans a chance to sell their crafts, such as handmade lace, to visitors from **Europe and North America.**

Victoria Falls, called Mosiatunya by local people, and the national park that surrounds the waterfall delight tourists who come from all over the world.

A sign at a game preserve warns of crossing elephants.

Courtesy of Tim Krieger

Independent Picture Service

Hwange National Park offers a home to these elephants of the *Loxodanta africana* species, who drink from the park's many watering holes.

A dry riverbed illustrates Zimbabwe's need to carefully conserve its water resources.

Lake Kyle, created by the construction of the Kyle Dam, lies in south central Zimbabwe and waters parts of the Low Veld.

Hydroelectric Power

With Zimbabwe's long dry season, water conservation is of major importance. Zimbabwe ranks high among tropical-zone countries in the number of dams it has constructed to collect water during peak rainfall periods for use throughout the year. Along with the Kariba hydroelectric complex on the Zambezi River, Zimbabwe has constructed a number of other major dams. Dams also store water for domestic and industrial uses for all the major population centers in Zimbabwe.

Large-scale irrigation projects on the Sabi River required a series of dams to be constructed to regulate the flow of water. Another dam, which was connected to the ARDA settlement schemes, was erected at Antelope. The dam that created Lake Kyle, the country's second largest lake, irrigates the Low Veld. One of Zimbabwe's earliest irrigation undertakings—in the Mazoe Valley—is still supplied with water from a dam built in 1920.

In addition to the major dams, many smaller ones have been constructed on farms, at mines, and near villages throughout Zimbabwe. Water provided by these small structures is used in homes and gardens to irrigate crops, to water livestock, and to breed fish.

The Future

Despite the struggle for black liberation in Zimbabwe, Mugabe's government has shown fairness in dealing not only with the white population but also with black politicians, who sometimes have used violence to oppose his policies. Although he has moved his country toward a one-party, socialist system, Mugabe has overseen a moderate program for Zimbabwean development. This plan encourages both national and international investors.

Zimbabwe faces the difficult task of balancing the rising expectations for jobs, land, and better wages against the national needs for austerity and continued economic stability. Fortunately, regional tensions among Zimbabwe, South Africa, and Mozambique have lessened. South Africa has extended citizenship to its majority black population, and civil conflict in Mozambique has eased. These developments have allowed Zimbabwe's government to focus on domestic issues. The government has succeeded in providing basic health and education to the majority of Zimbabweans. Much remains to be done, but the people of Zimbabwe can be optimistic about their country's future.

Courtesy of Tom O'Toole

Independence has brought Zimbabwe's younger citizens the possibility of a better standard of living. This possibility has pressured Robert Mugabe's government to satisfy black expectations, which largely have been ignored for many decades.

Index